RELEASE

the

PAUSE BUTTON

How to get Unstuck

Dr. Kathy H. Hubbard

WESTBOW
PRESS®
A DIVISION OF THOMAS NELSON
& ZONDERVAN

WestBow Press books may be ordered through booksellers or by contacting:

WestBow Press
A Division of Thomas Nelson & Zondervan
1663 Liberty Drive
Bloomington, IN 47403
www.westbowpress.com
844-714-3454

Scripture taken from the King James Version of the Bible.

Scripture taken from the New King James Version® Copyright © 1982
by Thomas Nelson. Used by permission. All rights reserved.

ISBN: 978-1-6642-7544-7 (sc)
ISBN: 978-1-6642-7545-4 (hc)
ISBN: 978-1-6642-7543-0 (e)

Library of Congress Control Number: 2022915162

Print information available on the last page.

WestBow Press rev. date: 11/10/2022

Special thanks to:

- God, my heavenly Father, who made it possible for me to accomplish this dream. I give God all the honor and praise.
- my husband, Johnny Hubbard, who has supported me throughout this entire project. He has been patient, loving, and kindhearted during this process and gave me the time and space I needed to complete this book.
- my children, Marneze Walker and Aris Hubbard, who have never given up on me. They continue to push and inspire me.
- Nicosia, Jarvis, Jasmine, Quaneisha, and Bryan for always supporting me.
- My parents, the late Samuel Head Sr. and Overseer Stella L. Head, who have always inspired and believed in me. They have encouraged me to accept that God has equipped me with everything I need to complete my mission and assignment from God.
- my brother, Samuel Head Jr., who is an extraordinary pastor and spiritual encourager to me and always listens when I share my goals.
- my sister, Tunja Brand, who has pushed me, believed in me, and encouraged me to complete the assignment.

I'd also like to thank my mentors.

- Marshawn Evan Daniels of *ME* Godfidence
- Babbie Mason, The Inner Circle
- Danielle Leslie, Course from Scratch
- Dr. Baruti Kafele

I'd like to thank Westbow Press and my editors.

CONTENTS

PREFACE

I F YOU WERE PURSUING YOUR GOALS, PLANS, PROJECTS, or even a mission you felt was your purpose but stopped your work either before or after COVID-19, It's time to release the pause button.

You need to decide you will no longer let anything hinder you from moving forward in this season. Galatians 5:7 (NIV) states, "You did run well: who did hinder you that you should not trust in the truth."

Who hindered you from completing your goals, dreams, visions, and aspirations? The answers typically turn out to be things like procrastination, finance, lack of support from others, lack of confidence in self-worth, or maybe you're simply standing in your own way. You may have experienced a loss of interest in your project and failed to move forward with the assignment.

My goal is to help encourage you to release whatever it may be that's keeping you stuck. Nothing happens by sitting around hoping for it or moping because it didn't happen or by making excuses about why you can't get moving. People often say things like, "I wish the right person would see my gift to help me get going." The chance of that happening is slimmer than if you got moving yourself to make it happen.

Just hoping the right person will see you and extend an opportunity to lead you into your destiny will very seldom work, but it is possible to work and trust God to make it happen. The Bible states, Matthew 19:26 (NIV) Jesus looked at them and said, "With man this is impossible, but with God all things are possible." You must be diligent about putting yourself in front of the right people. God will reward those who diligently seek him. Remain actively engaged with your project to be rewarded for your work. Be present when the right opportunity presents itself. When I began creating my book and online courses, the Holy Spirit gave me more creative ideas as the project came together. Now I officially have a book and classes.

The Bible states, James 2:26 (KJV) For as the body without the spirit is dead, so faith without works is dead also. You must have your work such as project, songs, press kit, books, and ideas put together before anyone in an executive position will look to help you. They will be able to better assess what you have and point you in the right direction as you continue working. I am simply saying that you shouldn't sit around wasting your life and time hoping the right person will come to you. You must put yourself before the right people, and have your package ready when you do so.

A good avenue to getting good help is seeking out mentors, consultants, leaders, and other professionals who can help point you in the right direction. Consider looking into mentors in your line of interest; see what they are doing that could help assist you with your project. You will be surprised to find conferences, tours, workshops, and even classes you can attend that will help you tremendously.

The best thing about searching out people who can help you is that they are there waiting for you to find them! If you are serious about moving forward, you should never let procrastination keep you from moving forward toward your destiny. You can't continue to stand back and watch others make it while you do nothing to help get yourself out of your rut. If you look at others and say to yourself, *I wish that could be me*, or *nothing big ever happens for me*, you will be off course for a long time. Take your mindset off others and prepare to walk in your destiny.

I was once talking to an older man named Willie Moore, and I told him I wished I had someone to tell me what to do in order to get my mission started and completed. He looked at me and said, "Kathy, you have to learn it and teach it to others." That was so profound to me. That's what I started doing. I admonish you to stop holding the pause button. That is what's hindering you from walking the path you desire.

When I was stuck procrastinating on this life journey, a world-renowned preacher named Bishop Neal Ellis from the Bahamas spoke a message, and it seemed as though he was speaking to me. He kept saying, "God has put you on a fast track to a victorious life in Him." Hearing that message motivated me to get started on the plan I wanted to pursue. I understood that being put on a fast track to a victorious life in God meant that for all the years I'd lost sitting around doing nothing while knowing I had an assignment to fulfill, God would give me another chance to work on my projects and complete them. He would help me get it done despite the time I'd lost.

Opportunities began happening for me. Since then, God has allowed me to write and record songs. I had an opportunity to interview and sing on television, on the *Sarah Hurd Show* on channel 57. He has allowed me to become a preacher and a leading lady in ministry to other women. He has allowed me to create online classes for women stuck in procrastination. He has also allowed me to write this book. Psalm 37:4 (KJV) says, "Delight yourself in the Lord, and He will give you the desires of your heart."

In your walk on this journey to destiny, remember to always put God first and seek him for direction and clarity; then, your goals, dreams, mission, project, or whatever it may be that you are pursuing will begin to unfold. Isaiah 65:24 (KJV) states, "And it shall come to pass, that before they call, I will answer; and while they are yet speaking, I will hear."

The Holy Spirit inspired me to write *Release the Pause Button* in order to deal with procrastination, distractions, and delays so that you may complete your mission, vision, purpose, or project. I have chosen to use a tape recorder as my main instrument, used for playing and recording music. I will use this instrument to compare the process of any mission or project you may be working on to help you out of places where you may have gotten stuck, which hindered you from completing your journey. As you reference the tape recorder to compare the process of your project, mission, or purpose, it can demonstrate how you can get started and move through your process. The buttons referenced consist of the play button, record, rewind, fast forward, pause, and stop. I will reference this device and its functioning buttons several times throughout the book as an example to help you understand steps you will possibly encounter while working on completing your project. I will give a brief description of each button throughout the book.

I pray this book gives you information that motivates you to move forward. I want to help you get unstuck and begin your project again. I am here to help you get through those tough spots you may be encountering. Don't let procrastination or anything else hold you hostage from pursuing the mission you have been called to complete.

ACKNOWLEDGMENTS

I WANT TO THANK MY MENTORS, MARSHAWN EVANS Daniels, Danielle Leslie, and Babbie Mason. Procrastination had a grip on me for years, but after I met these intelligent and outstanding ladies, things began to change for me. They have shared impactful information I needed to help get me through my process and complete it. I still have a few projects I'm working on, and now that I have the roadmap to follow from these ladies, I have confidence that I will accomplish the tasks set before me.

We should be willing to learn and work on things that help make us better and help others. I want to shine the light on these mentors a little more. Marshawn is an incredible mentor, excellent speaker, awesome leader, and coach, as well as CEO of her institution Godfidence. Danielle Leslie is a young, dynamic mentor who started an online business titled Course From Scratch. I tell you, she is a fabulous firecracker who will get the fire burning in your life. When

I started listening to her, she drew my attention to what she said and ignited me to pick up my story and tell it to others.

Babbie Mason is another mentor who has encouraged me along my journey. She has such a pleasant and teachable voice. When I joined her inner circle, she taught me many vital things about my voice, especially how to use and train it to work effectively for myself. Things like exercise, giving it rest and practicing warm-ups, and not eating and drinking things that are harmful to my vocal cords. Most importantly, all of these mentors spoke about telling your story and sharing your pain point.

I want to give thanks to Mr. Baruti Kafele, a former principal who presently serves as a leadership consultant. As COVID-19 shut the nation down, I was truly blessed by listening to him. He focused on school leadership and how to be a better leader. Mr. Kafele has poured a tremendous amount of wisdom into my life, my thinking, and my perspective. He has impacted my life in regards to my understanding of what a principal is. I am not a school leader and may never become one, but I have learned some valuable lessons from Mr. Kafele as a leader in education. Although I am not a principal, I will continue to endeavor as a church leader, youth leader and a leading lady for women. I feel that I've experienced many struggles people go through in their lives, as a child, an adult, and a woman, and I've overcome nearly all of them. I am here to help you get unstuck.

INTRODUCTION

During and after COVID-19

MY FRIEND, IF YOU HAVE BECOME STUCK AND ARE distracted from completing a project, mission, or purpose in life that you desire to pursue, I encourage you to *release the pause button*, and get started. It's time for you to be free from those distractions and delays. The year 2020 came in with many adversities for our nation, which added huge distractions and delays. The nationwide pandemic caused by an outbreak of the novel coronavirus COVID-19 snuffed out the lives of hundreds of thousands of loved ones. This pandemic left millions of people who'd been diagnosed with the virus still trying to recover. Even in 2022, the time of this writing, we still have people losing their lives to this monster. Many lost their jobs, families, liberties, and relationships. Schools and businesses alike shut down.

December of 2021 brought another variant, known as Omicron, and people had to practice social distancing once again. Churches were being closed. Almost everything you could think of came to a halt. These obstacles brought our nation and others unwanted challenging times.

Other horrible things were taking place in the country during the pandemic. Many innocent people were killed at the hand of the guilty, which led to massive protests across the United States. On top of these horrific events, a tremendously important election for our nation was approaching. With all this said, many books could be written on each of these momentous issues alone.

Our nation is in an uproar and puzzled, trying to figure things out and pull ourselves back together to heal. Second Chronicles 7:14 (NIV) says, "If my people, which are called by my name, shall humble themselves, and pray, seek my face and turn from their wicked ways; then will I hear from heaven, and will forgive their sin, and will heal their land."

We have to trust God and let him give us peace amid the storm. Despite the horrible things that have happened, there has been some good to come from it. The years of 2020 and 2021 gave people a rude awakening. They also allowed us to slow down in this fast-moving world and work on projects we'd placed on hold. It gave people a chance to refocus. It gave some people time to sit down with family members to eat, pray, talk, work, or whatever it may have been. COVID-19 has also had a tremendous impact on the professional world. In fact, with this multitude of issues this has been a *historic* time.

Because of everything that has happened, directly or

indirectly, many of us have been on pause with our lives, jobs, dreams, goals, missions, purposes, and more. We have to learn to live with this monster and move on with life. It's time to pick yourself up, gather the broken pieces, stop procrastinating with your dreams, and release the pause button.

CHAPTER ONE

Time to Release the Pause Button

I T'S TIME TO RELEASE THE PAUSE BUTTON. IT'S TIME TO get the mission accomplished. God has equipped you with everything you will need for this journey. It's time to let who you are rise and shine. The journey is achievable but tedious. The journey to accomplishing your mission is adventurous but rewarding when completed. I will use a tape recorder as an instrument throughout this book to help illustrate and identify different stages you are more than likely to encounter during the process of your project, mission, or purpose. A tape recorder is an electrical device used to record and play music or any information recorded on a cassette tape. Each function performs a different and vital task on the electronic device. First, let's talk about the pause button. The pause button is a function that's engaged only when pressed down, which is holding everything up on your mission. Selecting other buttons on the device allows you to perform the following procedure to get you started with your project.

In life, we go through many stages, milestones, obstacles, and phases to arrive at appointed places. Therefore, if you strive to reach a particular destiny, you must be ready to go through a process. You will have to make critical decisions throughout this informative context to take the proper steps toward your destiny; you have to be prayerful to make choices that will help you move toward your desired outcome. Most of the time, it's not easy to make decisions, so you should always consult with God. Proverbs 16:3 (KJV) tells us, "Commit thy work unto the Lord, and thy thoughts shall be established."

You may have already chosen a book, song, mission, business, or project to pursue; get focused on it, complete your project, and launch it. There are many ways to begin and complete your project or mission. I have been led in my spirit to write and inspire you to get started and complete your project. Once you have established your vision, you are now ready to work toward making it take off.

Be mindful that a description of the function of each part of the tape recorder will be analyzed to help you align your mission and have a good idea of what your journey should mimic. Throughout this book, you will better understand how this instrument applies to your assignment. The rewind button on the tape recorder allows you to go back to review the information you have already recorded. It represents the past. The rewind function sometimes verifies that you are not ready to progress forward. Next, the fast forward represents the future. Fast forward allows you to go ahead to add new information, new ideas, coverage, or review. This function helps confirm that you are ready to advance with your work. You are prepared to press rewind, fast forward, or play for another position as you release the pause button. They are all vital functions. When selecting essential parts of your project, such as notes, data, and recordings, you should go over your work to make sure the pieces you have collected or recorded make sense. When you release the pause button, you are ready to begin putting your project together. If you have created a project or mission and stopped because of distractions, you must find a place to start again. It would help if you worked diligently through your process, with the mindset that I must finish this project. Completing your project, mission, or destiny is the most important thing about starting the journey. However, keep in mind that you have the rewind and fast forward buttons, which will allow you to go backward or forward to inject material you may have omitted or if you have new things to add. Please take the opportunity to go back through your information, parts, and pieces, and select essential items that are vital to your project. Don't hit the stop button on the tape recorder; you have to keep moving. At this stage in the project, you should have a clear idea of what direction you are moving. It is possible to feel a little overwhelmed, but I encourage you to stay on task and keep pushing through this journey.

I'm reminded of the story in the bible about Moses and the children of Israel, how God had given them authority to go and possess the promise land. Yet they wandered around in the wilderness for 40 years murmuring and complaining instead of moving forward with the mission that God had given them to possess the land of canaanan which flowed with milk and honey. People above the age of 20 died out including Moses and Aaron because of disobedience and they didn't move forward with the assignment to go possess the land. If God has given you an assignment you must stop procrastinating and move forward. You must possess whatever aspiration, goal, dream, or mission God has given you the authority to possess. Don't let anything stand in your way.

CHAPTER TWO

Faith and Hard Work

MANY BLOCKAGES MAY HAVE HINDERED YOU FROM getting where you need to be and could be stopping you right now. A blockage is anything and everything that's underneath the pause button. For example, let's consider some things that are blockages: *I'll finish it next year, I don't have the money right now, I'm too busy, I'm*

too tired, I have too many things going on right now, I'll start when my children are older, I don't have time, I'm too old or too young, and so forth. All of these excuses can stop you.

Please do not allow procrastination to continue holding you hostage and pressing the pause button down. Procrastination wastes time that could be well spent on your project. The old saying "Nothing from nothing leaves nothing" is very true. It would be amazingly pricey if we add up the cost of wasted and lost time in our lives because of procrastination.

James 2:26 (NIV) says, "For as the body without the spirit is dead, so faith without works is dead also." Therefore, if faith without works is dead, if you aren't working, then your ideas, goals, dreams, and visions are deadly potential. You've got to work to get that blockage out of your process, or you will never see your destiny manifested.

While you are hard at work on your dreams, goals, visions, projects, or missions, you must have the patience to see all your work come together. A good activity to participate in that will help bring your project together is journaling. Journaling is essential because it helps you keep up with your thoughts. It helps you grow from what you have learned, and it helps you increase your wisdom as you review what you've done.

It would help if you journal any time you think of good ideas or when God lays something on your heart. You can journal whenever you have a large amount of information you're thinking about that you may not be able to remember. Be ready to journal when you're getting ready to go to bed, when ideas start running through your head. Journal when you are researching information.

The journaling process takes time, but you must be willing to do it because otherwise, you won't remember a lot of essential information. It would help if you recorded any answers to questions you find. For example: If you could answer the question, *what is my why?* It would be helpful to journal the solution. *What is my story?* You should continue to work diligently, trust God during the process, and have faith as he leads you through the process.

Hebrews 11:6 (KJV) states, "But without faith, it is impossible to please Him: for He that cometh to God must believe that he is and that He is a rewarder of them that diligently seek Him." Often a person's mission or project from God starts with thoughts, goals, and visions of the desired outcome, and when those are focused on, one must begin taking notes and recording. The things I had to do to begin my process were: break my cycle of procrastination, change my mindset, and invest in a mentor to help me get through.

I had to focus on the process ahead of me. I started journaling and recording what I heard in my spirit. I still have a habit of keeping a notepad with me in my purse and my nightstand to write things down that come to mind when I'm meditating on my goals. I also used my phone as a quick resource when I needed to record thoughts or take photos. You must begin recording and journaling everything you hear in your spirit that aligns with your mission.

While I was focusing on my project, there were many moments when the Holy Spirit spoke to me, and I was able to record it because I had my tools accessible. Whenever I didn't record my thoughts in that moment I would forget the information, and it never came back to me. So please try to keep a notepad with you. Don't worry if everything is not quite clear or if it's incomplete. Record, and it will soon make sense when you begin pulling things together.

Even if you are in bed and begin to hear something, you should get up and record it right away. I usually hear the best ideas when I'm lying down—calm, resting, and focusing on God. Keep everything together or in a specific place so you don't lose any of your thoughts and experiences encountered throughout your process. Proverbs 16:3 (KJV) says, "Commit thy work to the Lord, and thy thoughts shall be established."

Everyone should have a story to tell. When the time comes for you to pull all your pieces of information together, you should begin to organize your notes to be plain and easily understood. Habakkuk 2:2 (KJV) says, "And the Lord answered me, and said, Write the vision; and make [it] plain upon tables, that he may run that readeth it." After making your vision plain, you must run with it. Start working to see your vision and purpose manifest and come to fruition. You can't allow all of this good information to sit on your desk or in your mind.

My mentor Marshawn Evans told me that God's purpose for me is not only for me but also for others to benefit. Therefore, if God has given me a story or testimony, I shouldn't keep it to myself but should share it so others can see a path to overcome and follow their plans to get their desired outcomes. In Matthew 25:14-29 the Bible speaks against burying talents God gives us—especially if they could help us or others become better. When we share, God will bless us even more.

Don't stay stuck in procrastination but begin working on your dreams or projects. The process can take months and years if you stall. Make sure you don't put the project down haphazardly; you want to be careful not to form a poor habit of starting and stopping. The enemy wants to get you off course. Remember, faith without works is dead, and the longer you take to get it done, you will find yourself sitting while your purpose fails to manifest into reality. First Corinthians 15:58 (NLT) states, "Therefore, my beloved brothers, be steadfast, immovable, always abounding in the work of the Lord, knowing that in the Lord your labor is not in vain ."

Your whole process looks big to you and may seem as though you can't accomplish it, but you can achieve it. Work while it is day because when the night comes, no man can work. God put everything inside of you that you'll need to become who you're supposed to be. You have to get your mission, your project, completed. Jeremiah 1:5 (KJV) states, "Before I formed thee in the belly I knew thee; and before thou camest forth out of the womb I sanctified thee, and I ordained thee a prophet unto the nations."

David knew he could slay Goliath. God gave him the tenacity inside to face and kill that giant. God has also given you the determination and killer instinct you need to face whatever your giant is. Whether you need to master or defeat your giant, God has given you the ability and authority to do so. You will have reasonable time to practice and work out kinks to get the project just right during the process. Before David slew the giant, he had opportunities to practice his skills. He used his skills in other encounters leading up to his big event with Goliath.

David experienced great success when he killed a lion and a bear. This prepared him for an even more significant moment of triumph for killing the giant. You will have time to get ready for your most incredible moment of accomplishment if you use it wisely. David had great courage and confidence to defeat this giant. You have to be courageous and have faith like David. You have to know that even if the odds look like they are against you, with the Lord on your side you can do anything. Philippians 4:13 (KJV) states, "I can do all things through Christ who strengthens me." Your task may seem like it is unachievable, but it's not. When it looks like your struggles will take you down, don't worry—they won't. You can do it because you have God on your side. First John 4:4 (KJV) says, "Ye are of God, little children, and have overcome them; because greater is he that is in you than he who is in the world."

God has called you to do the mission you have before you. Many may be able to do the assignment you have, but if God has given the purpose to you, you should pursue it, and He will help you. On this journey of life, there are so many similar missions that need to be done. When you don't act on the assignment He has enlightened you to do, you should not point fingers at others in judgment, saying they've taken your idea. It doesn't mean they took your vision; you didn't move soon enough. Therefore you may see someone else doing something similar to your goal, purpose, or plan. God is an awesome God, and He has many to work with.

God is not assigned to any single individual. He will meet with you, commune with you, share with you, and help you, but He's not going to play with you or go back and forth. God's capabilities are so sovereign that he can most assuredly help you get it all done. He is not going to deal with double-minded folks who can't decide. He won't always wait until you know you're ready to move forward. You must step out in faith when God tells you too so that you don't get sidetracked by the enemy speaking negative things in your ear. The enemy may say things like, *You can do it next year,* or, *This project is too big for you.* Maybe even things like, *You don't have enough money,* or, *You need more experience.* The word of God tells us the danger of being double-minded. James 1:8 (KJV) says, "A double-minded man is unstable in all his ways." That's why you shouldn't allow the enemy to get between you and what God is leading you to do. If you're in that stage, you are still in an unstable season of your process. I want to encourage you with the word of God, which tells us in Proverbs 3:6 (KJV), "In all thy ways acknowledge Him, and he shall direct thy paths." This scripture convinces me to understand that God wants us to believe him so He can direct our paths.

Matthew 22:14 (KJV) says, "Many are called, but few are chosen." My mentor Marshawn Evans Daniels quotes this often, saying, "Many are called, but few are chosen; the ones who choose to step up and answer the call are the ones who are chosen." That is a compelling clause. There are so many people confused about their callings—confused about whether or not they are chosen. The statement that Marshawn Evans Daniels mentioned makes it straightforward for anyone to know whether he or she is called or chosen. If you keep wrestling with your decision and are constantly in doubt about your mission, if you keep second-guessing yourself, you will have reservations about stepping up to the plate.

You are going to remain in the "many are called" group. Sometimes you can miss your season and time because of too much waiting, laziness, procrastination, or lack of a positive mindset. The way you'll know you are stuck is by noticing that you keep dealing with the same things each time you try to get started up. You've never moved from that spot where you left off. *You are stuck!* You have to break that cycle. I say to you, "Rebuke that cycle of doing nothing." It's time to release the pause button. I encourage you to keep praying. That is the key to getting a lot of blockage out of your way. Praying is the key to getting you started and keeping you motivated and on track. Come on! It's time to get moving.

Referring back to the tape recorder—are you at a point of rewinding, fast-forwarding, recording, or playing? And in case we forgot about it, my suggestion is to never use the stop button. The fast-forward button will help you know if you are progressing; the stop button will make you aware you're at a standstill; the rewind button will let you go back. You have the record buttons, and if you press play and record at the same time, you can record information for your project. The play button will allow you to listen to what you have recorded during your process and what your work looks like at the completion stage.

Below are phases I followed to help keep me on track as I began writing this book and creating webinars to help women.

Phase 1: Approach
This stage can be compared to the pause button's release.

As you begin your journey on your particular project or mission, you must have the materials, variables, or thoughts ready to start your pursuit. You must be patient and diligent when getting your instructions, steps, and information. The approach phase can be very critical. This is the stage where I begin using my notes and other information I've recorded and collected. The approach phase is where you can start working on the project you have. You can begin by pulling out all your data, information, reports, surveys, and lyrics from your CDs, journals, phones, videos, or whatever you may have. Be patient because these phases can take a while.

Phase 2: Attack
This phase is when you press the fast-forward button.

In this period, you must work on your task rigorously. For example, if you have written a song, at this point you'll begin to sing it, put music to it, and lay your tracks. Keep practicing until it is just as you want. If you are writing a book, lay your chapters out and begin documenting everything from cover to cover. Do as much proofreading and editing as your knowledge will allow you to comprehend. Get your project or plan as perfect as possible to move to the next phase. You may have to press rewind during this stage to see or hear what you have stored in your recorder, book, or project. You will need to proofread, change or add to your project. This is the process that I followed for writing my book.

Phase 3: Follow-Through

Here you're pressing the play button again.

When you are in the follow-through phase, you can put it in the hands of a publishing company, producer, or business. You can view the development stages of your project as it progresses to completion. For example, this is the stage where the professionals will allow you to listen to the music you have created or the book you have written, or even the business you have developed before it advances to the final stage with the publisher, producer, or executive. At this point, one can put that final touch on the work.

Phase 4: Continuation of the Follow-Through to the Finish

Your project is in its final stage. The project is complete, and you are now ready to play and listen to or read the official copy of your work. At this stage, you will be ready to be the person you've worked so hard to become. You will be able to access the hard copy in your hand as a finished work, project, or business. This stage is your desired outcome.

As I close this chapter out, keep in mind that practical work will help you get there. God has taken steps with you to get you where you are. This process may seem complex and undoable, but you *can* do it. God wants you to prosper, and you must not stop working. Yes, you have walked through many of your steps, and the closer you get to your breakthrough or destiny, the more challenging it will get. You have to realize that at this point, you will be so close to completion that your hard work and dedication are the only things that will take you over into the beginning of your breakthrough.

Stop thinking you will make it with little to no work. Faith without work is dead. When you are in a process, you must realize that dedication and hard work catapult you to a finished product. The effort you put forth on your project will develop into your desired outcome. Don't think for a moment that you can't complete your goal, because you can. If I did it, you can too. As long as you work effectively and think clearly, the pieces will come together.

My biggest problem in getting a project to completion hasn't been finance, decision-making, or problem-solving, but procrastination and laziness. To keep the project moving, you must get rid of those hindrances. When you can defeat giants like those, you will be well on your way. Being a diligent worker and leader at what you do does not mean working hard for one day but working hard every single day. When you are working effectively daily, you are producing the expected outcome.

CHAPTER THREE

Inspiring Motivators

HAVING A MENTOR COULD BE A VITAL FACTOR IN helping you develop into the person you are seeking to become or helping you create the project you want to complete. I have several mentors who helped me along the way; they inspired and motivated me to stop procrastinating and get busy. Sometimes we need motivators to help us move out of the pause mode. As I share my testimony, I hope to inspire you to be active.

I was sitting at my home on a cold, snowy day, and I began

to surf the internet looking for ways to improve my skills and ran across Marshawn Evans Daniels. When I pulled this young lady up and started reading about her and listening to videos of events she had spoken at, I was truly inspired. It was what I needed to hear and exactly what I was looking for to give me a boost. She gave me so much confirmation that I felt she was talking directly to me when she spoke. She talked about how you can get paid for speaking by sharing your story. I sought her out and found out where I could attend one of her events. I found a tour in Atlanta. My son and I decided to participate in her workshop.

I was so impressed with her that I began keeping up with her and attending events regularly. I started investing in Marshawn shortly after she became my mentor. This young lady was an empowering speaker, full of knowledge and wisdom. She motivated me the day I met her to begin working on my project and not stop until I completed the work. I've had several projects since then.

The next mentor I came across was Babbie Mason, who inspired me in the music field to push forward and record a CD. She allowed me to perform a song at her Inner-Circle Conference. Babbie used a score sheet to evaluate her artists and gave me a score of one hundred on my musical performance.

Babbie taught classes on singing, using your voice effectively, performing, getting started in the professional world, and protecting your voice. She also had several guest speakers, including lawyers and authors. They spoke on writing books and songs and how artists should protect their work legally.

Finally, Danielle Leslie is another mentor to whom I've entrusted my time. She is known for teaching how to start a business and work from anywhere in the world. She also gave me one-on-one coaching and also offered group coaching with her head coach. She has online courses and a workbook for Course From Scratch. She inspired me to follow her guidance by starting my own business and having the ability to work from anywhere in the world.

A mentor can help walk you effectively through steps so you can get unstuck and get moving to reach your desired outcomes. You can perhaps seek a mentor who has already been where you need to go. Most mentors have the information you need to help you get started and be successful with your projects. After I attended my mentors' conferences, I continued following them on social media to stay updated. Many mentors have already experienced mountaintop experiences and roadblocks, which is why they help others. They can help make your transition smoother.

Since working with my own mentors, I myself have become an experienced mentor who works with everyday and professional women. I have several groups that I mentor, including a young adult women's group, a group at my church, and a mentor's group on Zoom. My mentors shared their story of transitioning from point A—a painful place, to point B—a good or successful place. Their stories encouraged me to share my story in order to help build a better culture. Mentors can assist in getting the right tools and information in your hands to help you establish your desired outcomes.

Mentors can often encourage you to push forward when you don't know what to do and find yourself at a standstill. A mentor can help you stay on task. When schoolchildren need help with lessons they don't understand, a teacher or tutor can help them understand and complete their work. Similarly, a mentor can be beneficial at helping you know what has caused you difficulties in your process. There's nothing wrong with having a mentor or a tutor—especially if he or she will help bring you to the next level.

Have you ever been looking on the internet or watching television—or even attending a conference—and suddenly heard someone speak out loud a vital part of a process or project that motivated you to get started? Well, that person or thing was there just for that moment to give you a boost, but a mentor is a person who will be there to walk you through your low and high points during the process.

The internet is a very resourceful tool in helping you find the type of mentor you would need, as you can type in the pursuits you're interested in and find leaders in those areas. You can find a myriad of mentors and read their information to see which one is the right fit for you. There are many types of mentors and information on the internet that can help anyone achieve his or her goals, but one has to be willing to pull up the search.

Various materials are very helpful to your project, mission, dream, or destiny, but you must spend time researching information. Marshawn had several books that encouraged women to work on themselves, including one called *Skirts in the Courtroom*. Danielle Leslie has a workbook called *Course from Scratch*. I love reading books that inspire me to work on my projects. Don't stop now; you are too close to walking in your destiny and purpose.

If you are planning on getting unstuck and moving ahead with your project, you may also want to consider having a brand if you don't already. A brand sets you apart from others; however, it can be unclear how you should choose your personal branding since you may have several ideas going on in your head at once. This particular step makes me think about a puzzle game that consists of connecting numbers. When connecting the numbers chronologically, it forms a picture you can't fully see until all the numbers are connected. When you join all the numbers, you may have a picture of an animal, a person, a building, or a figure. In the same way, when choosing a brand, you may have so many ideas you do not know what to use; however, when you continue to connect your thoughts and brainstorm, you will finally settle on a choice that will be perfect for your business. It will shape the brand you are looking to create.

I was right there—where you may be today. I had so many choices going through my head, but I kept writing them down, and I began to narrow my list down to the one that made the most sense for who I wanted to be and what I wanted my business to be. Your finished product should be what you're creating it to be. You are branding yourself, and you have to establish the best trademark to sell yourself.

My company's name is Speak 180, and my brand is Womentorial Consultant. I chose Speak 180 for my company's name because I speak to women who are stuck and even those who desire to be empowered by positive talk, hoping they'll make a 180 turn in the direction they wish to go to get their desired results. For example, I speak and then give action plans, road maps, and makeovers to help point ladies in the direction they're striving to move toward so they can accomplish their goals.

I created my Womentorial Consultant brand by combining the words *women* and *mentor* together to suggest I am a mentor for women and a consultant who can give advice they may need. I created the title *womentorial*. I've held a specialist degree in leadership and administration for over fifteen years and a doctorate in biblical ministry for over a decade; with these certifications, I am well qualified and equipped to lead, inspire, empower, and counsel women to move in the right direction to accomplish their goals.

I want to help you release the pause button. Let's elaborate on that small word (pause), which carries so much weight in this book. Pause means a temporary stop, wait, rest. It means to dwell, linger, or hesitate. It also means a break or suspension. Can you see yourself wrapped up in or wrestling with any of those words? As I said early, it's a small word but carries so much weight, and my reason for saying that is because pausing too long can hinder you from reaching your goal, mission, or dream in life.

Returning to the tape recorder metaphor, let's talk about the stop button. The stop button is worse than the pause. *Stop* means to block, cease from, leave off, or discontinue. It also means to obstruct, interrupt, restrain, or prevent from proceeding. Are you in any of those modes? I hope you're only on pause rather than stop, because if you are in stop mode, you've probably already tuned me out.

I can help you get out of pause mode, and I want to help you. I want to help provide my service because I was on pause and stayed there for years. It took me a long time to move forward and release myself to move forward. Regardless of the mode you're in, if you're holding the pause button down, you must snap out of it. Let go of that button and move forward. Your dreams will soon get old, your goals will quickly need to be refreshed or replaced, and your mission will become stagnated. It is disappointing to know that your thoughts and dreams are stale and need revamping or doing all over again. So let's get moving.

CHAPTER FOUR

Stay on Task

Y OU MUST STAY ON TASK AND BE IN ALIGNMENT WITH your goals. I kept dragging my feet about completing this book, and I did not take the time to pull my notes out to begin typing. I had the material and information already done, but I needed to organize my manuscript. Finally, one hot summer day, I chose not to let procrastination deprive me of completing my book anymore.

Once I began, I kept pursuing and attacking it and following through until I finished. You can't fully be who you are designed to be before your season. At this point, you can envision where you want to be eventually, but you have to walk it out step by step.

You should work hard before your season comes; then, you will be ready and equipped to walk into your destiny when your time arrives. Setting goals and due dates and sticking to them will help you stay on task. You have to work on something every day to be successful—even prayer.

There will be times when you will think, *I wish I could just meet the right person to help get me on track.* You have to keep working on it. If you allow me to help you through this process, you will make it if you stay on task. There is a step-by-step process I would like to help you follow that uses seven essential operations to help anyone become unstuck and eradicate complacency.

Seven Essential Operations to Eradicate Complacency

1. **Power on:** (Wake up) hastens, accelerate
   You need to wake up, make haste, and begin to accelerate. You have to be quick in your spirit and within yourself. You have been waiting and pondering on this particular project for too long. Time is of

the essence, and you can no longer be lazy or stuck. People are waiting to hear from you. God has given you a unique way to share your vision and plan with others. Come on and get started. The longer you wait, the longer it will take. Your work will inspire others to get started. It will not get accomplished unless you get it done. When you begin working it will eradicate complacency and wake up your desire to complete your project.

2. **Play:** (Work) performance, and journaling
   Your work ethic will determine how well you perform. When you are in work mode, journaling is one of the most critical objectives you can put into play. Journaling will open your mind to help you be more cognitive. It uncovers ideas and enables you to focus on your goals, solve problems, or at least find some solutions as you write. Think of journaling as writing a note to yourself. You can also record thoughts you consider when making a decision. You can use words to paint a picture or scene. Be creative if you would like! You could even make a list of quotations you find interesting.

   When I opened up my journal and looked at all the information I'd recorded, I knew I needed to work on sharing this information with others. I wrote several quotes in my journal that I wanted to put in my book. The Holy Spirit gave me the phases and steps to add to my book as I journaled. As I think back on how I wanted to get started with my project but didn't know where to start, I kept hearing people say to pray about it—some even said to make that jump—but nobody could give me a plan on how to do that.

I'm giving you the road map on doing your work, but *you* have to get it done. You will be surprised to look back at your journal and see some of the fantastic ideas you had. Please don't let it go to waste; come on, and share your work. I'd love to hear how this book helped or inspired you to get started.

"And the Lord answered me, and said, Write the vision and make it plain upon tables, that he may run that readeth it" (Habakkuk 2:2 KJV)

3. **Rewind:** Reverse to review

    Go back and reread what you've written. Reviewing a journal is done from a distance. You're looking back at your journaling work because it helps you learn about yourself and grow in wisdom. When you journal, you use your mind and reflect on your experiences so you can get more out of them.

    Keep working. Remember to do the things you need to do right now to eradicate complacency. Work while it's the day. Work while it's your season. If you have a copy of this book in your hand and are reading it, then it is your season.

4. **Fast-Forward:** accelerate, affirming, onward, or advance The more you fast forward, the more you will advance and approach your mission's end. You must accelerate with excellent approval and affirmation of your work. Moving onward is a perfect place to be. It helps catapult you to the completion of the process.

5. **Stop:** The stop button should never be considered in this process because it puts you in the mode of doing *nothing*!

6. **Record:** is considered all of the information you have journaled or recorded into your notebook, laptop, or cell phone. It's time to use what you have stored.

7. **Pause:** Release the pause button. Stamp out procrastination, and do it.

The next example can be viewed as a demonstration of the process you will have to go through to reach a successful end result. You must complete the process. The completed process is like cracked and shelled nuts already inside a sealed bag on the shelf in a grocery store. As I explain the process, a nut has to grow to become edible. It takes time for the process to happen, as a nut develops through time. It starts from a nut sown in the ground that germinates. Then it goes to a *seedling* stage. Next, it grows into a small tree. At this point, the tree is still young and has no nuts on it. This tree must be nurtured to grow large.

During your process, as time passes, this tree will become mature and ready to bare nuts. The nuts start at a green stage; then, they will eventually become ripe enough to harvest. The nuts are ready to be harvested, shelled, and enjoyed at this time and season. Those nuts become the product ready for packaging and marketing. When packaged, it is ready to be branded. These nuts can be packaged as nuts inside their shells or already shelled as whole nuts or pecan pieces. When the product is branded, it is ready to be sold. This example demonstrates the process you may go through during the stages of your journey.

I had the desire to be a professional performing artist, but I was not preparing myself to be that artist. I didn't plant the seed by practicing and persevering with it daily; therefore, I never achieved that goal. I did a lot of hit-and-miss projects.

Another opportunity came that allowed me to speak to women who were stuck in predicaments. I began taking this opportunity and gift seriously. I planted the plan, worked on it, practiced it, wrote it, and made it plain. It started growing and developing into a gift that others wanted to hear. I had to plant what I wanted to come up. I had to practice this gift, water this gift, work on it, and watch God give the increase. I am now teaching classes and leading others on how to get unstuck. God has manifested my gift of speaking and sharing information with others to help them manifest and grow.

Here's how you can compare the process mentioned

above to your project. You must have a product to plant. This means you should write your plan out. When you plant, or write down, your vision, it's not going to come up ready for others to see it right away. Your project will go through stages, and each phase is critical to the process. First you must water your dream, which helps it manifest. As it begins to grow, you should do some caregiving and nurture your vision. When you work on your vision to help it grow by allowing mentors to help you month after month you will eventually see it manifest.

Sometimes it takes a while for your vision to mature completely. When it becomes a fully grown tree, it will bare green nuts, which will soon ripen and be ready for harvest. When I started working on my projects and advertising my business, fruits began to show, and people began to seek after me for events. It was time to produce my product. After producing and completing the product, I had to decide whether or not I wanted to sell it or offer it for free. After this stage, it was time for a brand, because the process was finished, just like the nut.

As I branded myself, my work became appealing, and then I had a fully developed project. If you've created something desirable and done it well, it will sell. This brings me to the point of telling you to *release the pause button* and go from stuck to earning bucks—if that's your desire.

CHAPTER FIVE

Discipline Will Keep You

CONTINUE TO DO YOUR BEST, WORKING WITH efficacy and proficiency to complete your mission. You have to sell yourself; therefore, you can't afford to produce any junk. It takes perseverance to be (and remain) effective. To have discipline, you must have goals to follow. It is hard to pull out your work and labor on it every day. Goal setting and following through will help you keep moving along the process. You must have the tenacity to take the project on, revamp it, and complete it. Self-control plays a vital part in the process. It's effortless to be lazy, quit, or take breaks.

Cutting grass often helps the yard look great. When you allow the grass in your yard to grow for weeks, it looks bad. Working on your project helps it get better. It begins to look bad if you neglect to keep your work up with your project, and it can also make you look lazy. Setbacks may come from time to time, but you have to work through them. You have to find the strength to keep going. Setbacks often test your endurance. Obstacles will come to make you want to quit, but you will see a significant breakthrough and product if you can endure these overwhelming times.

The race is not given to the swift nor the strong but to those who take it to the end. In this case, work to complete your task or assignment. Understand that many have already started with you, and many will start without you. You have to do it and keep the discipline to stay on task until completing the entire project or assignment given. The word of God tells us in Philippians 4:13 that we can do all things through Christ who strengthens us. This lets me know that if I discipline myself to be obedient, I can do the things I desire to do.

If you prepare yourself with godly discipline, you shape yourself for success. Using godly discipline and self-discipline together helps shape you and keep you moving in the right direction. You will most definitely need good discipline to keep going. There was a time in my life when I used self-discipline as a tool to help me go back to college a couple of years after dropping out to work. Returning to school gave me the best practice of effectively using self-discipline that I had ever experienced. That was the beginning of my potential to work hard and remain focused on the courses I had before me.

As mentioned earlier, I'd dropped out of school for two years. After I realized how hard it was to get a decent career with just the two years I'd completed, I knew I must get back in school and work hard to finish. I didn't have the funds I needed, but I stretched what I had and made so many sacrifices. I didn't have people encouraging me at the time, so I knew this would be a journey of the self.

When I went back to the junior college I'd left, it was in the process of becoming a four-year college, but I was returning for my associate's degree. I had to commute every day for about an hour and thirty minutes one way. I encouraged myself every day by saying, *You will make it. Hang in there. It will pay off.* I also said to myself, *One day you will get this degree. After the associate's degree, you'll get the bachelor's degree; then, after that, you will get a master's. Next, you will receive a specialist degree.* I didn't stop there; I continued to think, *You will also receive a doctorate.*

I finished my associate's work at the junior college and then went to Georgia College in Milledgeville, Georgia. I kept speaking and prophesying those words over my life, and God performed it. He honored my hard work, self-discipline, and dedication to finish. He kept me every day as I commuted from each school I attended. I thought my accomplishments were the hardest things to complete, but I had to discipline myself and keep a good attitude, which made it easier to get them done.

I realized if I invested in myself the return would be great, and it has been. I've heard Donald Lawrence and the Tri-City Singers sing these words, "sometimes you have to encourage yourself, and sometimes you have to speak a word over yourself." That is very true. I would go so far as to say most of the time we have to encourage ourselves, because a lot of the time, no one else will encourage us.

Winter Season

People like to refer to winter as a time when things die, but I feel it is a perfect time to work hard and get a lot accomplished. There will be a time when you'll feel like you are in a dead season or need time off. I encourage you to believe and know that your off-season is the best time for your process and not the worst. How is this so?

Let's look at any athlete who has entered his or her off-season. A player could think, *Wow, I'm glad the season is over. I can get some rest.* After a long, arduous season, one needs a break from the driven, hard physical work of playing. But athletes need to transition into working on mechanical skills, which are needed to improve for the next challenging season. Sure, athletes need to repair their bodies and evaluate parts that need special attention. Dedicated players continue to work hard on techniques, skills, and goals during their off-season because this allows them to make things better and not lose momentum as they prepare to thrive in the future.

You have to practice hard during the off-season because this is when you will see your most significant improvement. Most of the time, it is not during the season that athletes get better, but during their off-season. The playing season is for conditioning, learning plays, and doing repetition drills. During the playing or working season of your business, career, or mission, you have to be prepared for speaking, playing, presenting, attending conferences, and so on. During the off-season you have to improve your speeches, PowerPoint skills, and knowledge; assess the company; evaluate yourself; and work toward improvement. Please don't consider the off-season as rest time, because if you do, you could remain in the same place you are after the season you just finished.

I want to discuss a self-management model I ran across that was created by the Malaysian Institute of Management. This model helps people understand the impact of self-management. I believe it will help any potential entrepreneur self-evaluate and move toward having a strong business foundation. I believe this model will be helpful as you work through your process. The model discusses ten self-management skills you can apply to any mission you may be working on, as well as a project or plan. It is hard to manage others well if you cannot manage yourself well. A Chinese proverb goes like this: "If you can command yourself, you can command the world." As a leader, if you are stumbling over your own weaknesses and misdoings you will find it hard to encourage others to improve.

The ten components of this self-management model will benefit those who are working on themselves or on a significant project. I shared this model because it will help you understand how and where to improve your skills for your business or project. If you know you are held hostage by procrastination or lost with little to no direction, this self-management model will help reveal how you can work to improve yourself, get moving, and work effectively.

KLSCC's Model of Self-Management

I will give you a summary of each of these self-management skills written by the Malaysian Institute of Management in 2012-04-21. They can be found at http://www360doc.com.

1. **Self-Awareness**
   Self-awareness is a vital skill to start with as you begin improving yourself. Before leaders can improve themselves, they must know the areas that need their attention. Uncovering mistakes, flaws, and

weaknesses can help leaders improve themselves. When leaders find out the truth about themselves, it serves them well—especially if they want to better themselves. It was recorded by the Malaysian Institute of Management that a leader who creates fear in others through intimidation and vengeful actions will discourage people from speaking the truth about himself.

2. **Self-Belief**

The next skill is self-belief. There is no one who will believe in you if you do not believe in yourself. The most significant power doesn't come from others believing in you but from whether you genuinely believe in yourself. When you believe in yourself, something magical happens.

A belief in yourself is a powerful force that will compel you to commit your thinking, feeling, and actions toward a goal. A strong enough confidence will overcome tremendous odds to help you achieve success. A good starting point to believing in yourself and your abilities is believing that God has created a superior being in everyone. We all have what is needed to achieve excellence. All that is required is believing in ourselves wholeheartedly and tapping into the inner resources of discipline, creativity, and resilience to achieve the extraordinary.

3. **Self-Responsibility**

   It's tempting to blame others when things don't work out the way we want them to. Some managers blame their subordinates for poor direction when they are not achieving much in the workplace. Others blame their staff for not cooperating with them or the industry and economy for their poor performance. Of course the ultimate excuse is to blame terrible fate or the whole world for failure.

   Playing the blame game is never productive, as nothing gets done. When we blame others for our plights, we genuinely surrender the power to change. We can give a thousand and one excuses for why we couldn't complete our tasks or achieve our goals; however, real value comes from taking responsibility for ourselves and making things happen.

4. **Self-Discipline**

   Many well-educated, bright managers are achieving less than their potential in the workplace. They lack the self-discipline to perform to the level required for their position. Self-discipline is necessary for staying focused to complete tasks within a given time frame, quality standard, and budgeted cost.

   Achieving excellence in whatever work you do requires self-discipline. As much as an athlete requires the self-discipline to train for excellence in world-class competitions, managers need to have the self-discipline to learn and master knowledge and skills to achieve world-class standards in their work.

Plato said it best: "The first and best victory is to conquer self." Managers need to conquer apathy, negative thinking, procrastination, delay, complacency, favoritism, and a host of other unproductive habits, all of which require self-discipline.

5. **Self-Motivation**

Without motivation, a manager will go about his work stagnant. He would not have the energy and enthusiasm to bring out the best of himself at work. At best, he will perform mediocre work that barely meets the requirements at the workplace. While there is nothing wrong with being motivated by a kind encouragement and even a reward for good performance, waiting to get inspired before getting things done is putting the cart before the horse. The problem with depending on others for motivation is that the quality of the work done will not be consistent.

The best way to ensure top-quality work is to practice self-motivation in getting things done. Self-motivation comes from within, and the driving force is the realization that the best rewards come from the sense of satisfaction of having given one's all to achieve the best. What one does with the best effort creates excellence. The creation of excellence and its results become the critical motivation. Self-motivated ones should not worry about rewards because diligent work with excellence eventually gets recognized.

6. **Self-Resourcefulness**

There are limits to money, human resources, machines, materials, and time; however, there are no limits when we tap into our inner resources, like creativity. Before humans invented sophisticated lifting machines, the speed of moving heavy things from one place to another depended on how many men were available. As humans became more creative, however, they invented wheels and pulleys to help them move heavier things with fewer people. They could do this because they had managed to tap into their creativity and thus came up with equipment to help achieve more output with less input.

Likewise, in the modern workplace we need thinking leaders who will tap into their creative ideas to achieve more with less. And this requires self-resourcefulness. One can shorten a working process, find a solution to a problem in a shorter time frame, create new services, or find new ways to win customers, increase market share, and stay competitive.

7. **Self-Achievement**

It's great to have a team of people working together to achieve collective results, which has greater value than individual results. The value of a team is the synergistic effect it provides—other than the fun of working with others, of course. Even within a group, though, each individual must contribute and can therefore find self-achievement in a group effort, providing a sense of satisfaction.

One certainly does not live on bread alone. With self-achievement comes the reinforced self-belief and motivation to spur one to greater heights. Thus, in building a team, a leader needs to chalk up his accomplishments as he encourages others to succeed.

8. **Self-Monitoring**

No one can monitor you better than yourself. You are the best person who will be at the right time and the right place to know whether you are about to do something you aren't supposed to or are supposed to do something you're not. Self-monitoring is not only more timely and practical but also less stressful. Imagine being monitored by others around the clock! Employees who do not undertake self-monitoring often show up late for work or official functions. They miss deadlines or do work that is not up to expectations. People, who undertake self-monitoring to achieve better results, feel better about themselves because they avoid having others monitor them.

9. **Self-Correction**

Many people wait for mistakes to be discovered and pointed out for correction. While it seems easier for an employee to do work and pass it on to the superior to spot and correct errors, it is also less commendable. To stand out as an extraordinary manager, it will serve to undertake self-correction before handing work over to the superior. Self-correction is a habit that can be useful. All it requires is paying a little more attention to combing through homework to ensure errors or omissions are corrected early before someone else discovers them.

10. **Self-Learning**

Companies may organize regular formal training or briefing sessions for their staff; however, there is no learning more effective than self-learning. There are many ways people can go about understanding self-learning. For instance, they can ask those who already know or have prior experience. They can also read books or obtain relevant sources of information regarding a specific topic of relevance and interest. Today, with the advent of the internet and the accessibility to so many knowledge portals, there is no excuse for an executive or leader not to undertake self-learning. This self-management skills model was developed by the Malaysian Institute of Management. Though the model focused more on leaders, I believe anyone who's on a mission to achieve a goal, mission, or plan can glean helpful information from this model.

I will sum up this chapter by saying: The truth is that we know ourselves better than anyone, even specific areas we lack in and which modes of learning will be most effective for ourselves.

Actor and martial-arts expert Bruce Lee once said, "I have come to discover through earnest personal experience and dedicated learning that ultimately the greatest help is self-help. There is no other help but self-help—doing one's best, dedicating oneself wholeheartedly to a given task, which happens to have no end but is an on-going process."

CHAPTER SIX

No Backtracking

WHILE WORKING ON YOUR PROJECT, YOU MAY FEEL overwhelmed. You may feel you've bitten off too much. As I began to approach the middle of an online course I'd created for stuck women, I felt like I had bitten off too much. I had gotten to where I couldn't finish the project because I had too much going on with work, with my church, and with community obligations. I felt like I was running into brick walls trying to make excellent videos and uploading empowering lessons on my coursework. I felt like I had gone as far as I could go on my own, but I honestly had not gone to the extreme. I was backtracking.

Then I figured out how simple the next step was to keep moving—I got busy again. Let me say this while exiting chapter 5; I had to go back several times to identify with the self-management model created by the Malaysian Institute of Management to help me get back on track and moving again. You can't let your inside voice speak negatively to you. Please don't allow skepticism to step in. I've had several times where I had a negative attitude or voice saying to me, *Forget about it. You're too old now. You're taking too long. You can't do this.* I've even spoken to myself and said, *Kathy, you're not doing anything!*

Don't look back. Keep moving forward; you will be too far to turn around at this point in your process. Keep pressing toward the finish line. God will give you the wisdom and patience to endure and finish what you have started. Don't lose focus on your project or dream. Please don't give up; it will happen. Keep the faith. Maxwell Maltz stated, "What is an opportunity, and when does it knock? It never knocks. You can wait a whole lifetime, listening, hoping, and you will hear no knocking. None at all—You are an opportunity, and you must knock on the door leading to your destiny" (https://www.goodreads).

John Richardson said, "When it comes to the future, there are three kinds of people: those who let it happen, those who make it happen, and those who wonder what happened" (https://etc.bdir.in/quotes/view/MjgwOTQ). Suppose your goal, destiny, or vision is something you've been working on, but somewhere along the way, you felt you couldn't finish it or didn't want to try. In that case, I guarantee you this is something you will regret for years and even a lifetime if you don't complete it. You'll look at others who did complete their projects and regret you didn't.

Don't leave your dream unfinished. It's tough to keep going on sometimes, but you have to find the willpower to get it done. Please release the pause button. Don't be left saying *I should have*, *I could have*, or *I would have*. Please see the process through.

Everyone needs to have a plan for accomplishing goals and then follow through with the project. Proverbs 29:18 (KJV) states, "Where there is no vision, the people perish: but he that keepeth the law, happy is he." If you feel you have a particular skill or ability and it seems others have looked you over for many years, now is your time to get your skill developed, sharpened, and working in full force. You have looked over your gifts or talents if you never get your project done.

Don't rely on others to recognize your talents if you're not acknowledging and perfecting your skills. No one else is obligated to recognize it. Sometimes it's possible that you've looked yourself over and won't give yourself the credit you deserve.

There were many times when I wanted to step out and move forward with my project and wanted others to encourage me to go forth, but I didn't get the approval I was looking to receive. I know God has blessed me with the gift of leadership, coaching and teaching, but I put myself on the back burner to push others forward before realizing there was no one encouraging me to where I was gifted to be. You have to do as John Maltz says and take the opportunity when it comes because it will not knock at your door. You are an opportunity.

I love this next parable that I will share with you, because it brings a little more clarity to why we should not hide our talents and why we should invest in them. Even though we speak of two different skills, I believe we can apply this principle the same way.

> For the kingdom of heaven is a man traveling into a far country, which called his servants and delivered unto them his goods. And unto one he gave five talents, to another two, and to another one; to every man according to his several abilities; and straightway took his journey. Then he that had received the five talents went and traded with the same and made them other five talents. And likewise he that had received two, he also gained other two. But the one that had received one went and dug in the earth and hid his lord's money. After a long time the lord of those servants cometh, and reckoneth with them. And so he that had

received five talents came and brought other five talents, saying, Lord, thou deliveredst unto me five talents: behold, I have gained beside them five talents more. His lord said unto him, well done, thou good and faithful servant: thou hast been faithful over a few things, I will make thee ruler over many things: enter thou into the joy of thy lord. He also that had received two talents came and said, Lord, thou deliveredst unto me two talents: behold, I have gained two other talents beside them. His lord said unto him, well done, good and faithful servant; thou hast been faithful over a few things, I will make thee ruler over many things: enter thou into the joy of thy lord. Then he which had received the one talent came and said, Lord, I knew thee that thou art a hard man, reaping where thou hast not sown, and gathering where thou hast not strawed: And I was afraid, and went and hid thy talent in the earth: lo, there thou hast that is thine. His lord answered and said unto him, Thou wicked and slothful servant, thou knewest that I reap where I sowed not, and gather where I have not strawed: Thou oughtest therefore to have put my money to the exchangers, and then at my coming I should have received mine own with usury. Take therefore the talent from him and give it unto him which hath ten talents. For unto everyone that hath shall be given, and he shall have abundance: but from him, that hath not shall be taken away even that which he hath. (Matthew 25:14–29 KJV)

This passage gives an excellent example of how that particular parable can be applied to our very own lives today—especially if we are having problems trying to figure out whether we should invest in ourselves. There are so many points that help clarify any mission, vision, goal, or dream you may be pursuing. You shouldn't hide your talents but recognize them and invest in them.

These particular verses speak of monetary talents. Still, I believe it can also help us better understand and clarify how to invest in our abilities. These scriptures can encourage us how we can expect a return on the investment when we invest. If you don't invest in your talent or gift, it cannot grow, multiply, or get better. Being unwilling to invest in what God has given you will lessen your chance of keeping the gift. I've heard people say that they used to sing, but since they never used their gifts, they couldn't sing like they used to.

Another point is that when you invest in what you have, it's possible to grow, multiply, and get better. Luke 12:48b (KJV) states, "For unto whomever much is given, of him shall be much required." If you have heard this particular scripture, it means we are held responsible for what we have been given. When God blesses us with talents, wealth, knowledge, and gifts, it is expected we use them, take care of them, and invest in them and bless others.

Hebrews 11:6 (NIV) states, "But without faith it is impossible to please Him, for he who comes to God must believe that he is and that He is a rewarder of those who diligently seek Him." Have faith as you work through your project.

This is another example of how investing in yourself gives you a great payoff. Have you ever looked at a before-and-after picture of someone's weight loss journey? I have been overweight before, and I've decided to do something about it. I joined the Weight Watchers program to lose some weight, and I was happy with the outcome. I reached my desired maintenance weight. I had to work hard to obtain that weight loss and not return to my heaviest weight. It took dedicated work and sacrifice. Once I reached my desired weight, I loved how I looked and felt. I loved what I had achieved. It inspired others around me to do the same.

What I would hope you get out of the weight loss scenario is that it doesn't matter what you are trying to achieve—it will take hard work, and dedication to do it. When you are in the middle of that process, things will look a little better, and you'll feel encouraged to work to the finish. When you have finished the process and see the outcome, you will be inspired, encouraged, and happy.

Rewinding moves backward to where you started. I

recommend you not participate in a tremendous amount of backtracking. Using the fast-forward button moves you toward the completion. Once you get your mission accomplished, it's up to you whether or not you want to continue moving forward to become an icon. If you have the determination and strength to finish the work, you will have the opportunity to become the model or finished product you desire to be.

CHAPTER SEVEN

Freezing

W HEN YOU'RE GETTING READY FOR YOUR FINISHED product to be debuted or showcased, you cannot freeze up. When releasing that long-awaited pause button you've been holding down, you can't go into panic mode. For example, with this tape recorder I've referenced throughout this book, the function button on this device could sometimes jam or freeze on you, but you must not panic.

For readers who are too young to know what a tape recorder is, I want to enlighten you on the details of this particular instrument. Sometimes buttons on a tape recorder would jam, and you'd have to keep pressing buttons until the right one would make the jammed button pop up. Responding to this problem, you shouldn't keep tapping on the wrong buttons to get the one you want unstuck. Don't panic! If this situation ever happens in a church or at a big event, you could troubleshoot the problem or have someone in place to help get it resolved quickly.

I once saw this type of problem happen in church with a soloist. The singer was preparing to perform with an accompanying track. As she walked up on stage, the sound technician had the pause button pressed down, waiting to release it. As the singer stood up to the microphone, the sound tech pressed the play button, but no sound came out. The sound technician had to go back and check for any mistakes he may have made that were preventing sound from playing.

The singer immediately began to get a little agitated because she had nothing else prepared. Suddenly the technician realized the volume was muted. He sighed with relief, rewound the track, and turned the volume up to unfreeze the moment of silence. I said that to say, when your showcase moment comes, you have to be ready to shine. Being prepared to shine means you have to have everything ready to perform, even if you need a backup in place. You can't help making a few mistakes, but always be prepared to do your best and have a backup.

When you put yourself in front of the right people, you need a firm delivery. It doesn't matter what project you may be working toward or what you may be working on; be ready. Matthew 22:14 (KJV) states, "Many are called but few are chosen." I believe the chosen are the ones who decide to get everything in place and the ones who work hard to be ready for whatever calling lies ahead. Preparation and hard work are two things needed to complete your plan.

It's hard to do an excellent job at anything when you are not ready and prepared. T. D. Jakes, a renowned preacher, repeatedly states these simple words over and over again: "Get ready! Get ready! Get ready." I believe preparation helps you be effective with the calling God has ordained for you. Do not expect to step in front of anyone with your products unprepared. Therefore, you must get ready! How can you tell an expert that you have some products that are not complete? Do you expect them to take partial work? Prove yourself to be ready for the call. In other words, study to show yourself approved.

Distraction and Delays

If you get distracted or delayed from your track, you have to get yourself refocused quickly. Sometimes when you're dealing with too many incomplete thoughts and ideas or loose ends, you can quickly get distracted, get off track, and be delayed.

For example, I've had so many different ideas and thoughts on my phone and notepad dealing with other projects, and they confused me because I tried to run them all together to make it work for one big project. That won't work because you can make the project too broad and not really hit the nail on the head. You have to make sure pieces fit together. You have to constantly refer back to the origin of your why and your brand. When you have so many thoughts, ideas, talents, and abilities, you can get confused, which will delay your process.

You have to remain focused to brand yourself. Delaying and being distracted will have you procrastinating for a long time. Distractions are things that will throw you off track and keep you from getting to your destiny. These things make you feel like you have too much going on at once. They cling to you and make you feel like they take top priority over your work with your mission or project.

You have to work hard not to let distractions delay you because they will affect your progress and keep you from getting to your completion. When I started building my brand, I adopted this slogan that I mentioned earlier— *working on myself every day nonstop.* This slogan helped me focus and commit to doing at least one or two things with my project every day. I now use this slogan as my philosophy.

You have to do the same thing with your project; commit to making yourself work on your project every day, even if you don't do much. For example, take someone who wants a firm stomach but doesn't have it. He or she must work on it by exercising and working hard to get that flab to turn to abs. One has to realize that many things cause fat to grow on the stomach, and it will take a lot to get that fat off.

Look at your project or mission. You can let too many ideas, thoughts, and other things get in your way to the point that they cover up your mission, which makes it unclear what you are even working on. You have to get those things out of your way. I want to compare a tremendous abdominal muscle to a great brand, but imagine your ab muscle is covered with fat (distractions). You get rid of the fat by using a step-by-step process. When you exercise and work that muscle until you begin to see inches and even pounds coming off, you'll start to see muscles developing.

I got through delays and distractions by working on my business every day to get unstuck. As I stated earlier, I created this philosophy by working on myself every day, nonstop from the acronym WOMEN, which means that I will work on something every day that concerns my business—great or small. Creating something that will inspire you to work will help you stay focused and intense at working on your project. I was able to use this saying as a tool to help me during my struggles and accomplishments as I moved forward with my project.

Too many ideas, thoughts, and things can stop your work and make branding unclear. When you begin to methodically move those things out of the way to uncover your potential brand, your choices will become more apparent. Maybe you have several things on your mind that you are considering doing, like starting a business or an organization or becoming a particular kind of person—or whatever it may be. If you're trying to put all your thoughts together at once, I am sorry to tell you it's not going to work like that. Try narrowing those things down until you only have one or two things you're considering for your brand.

Once you have narrowed your clutter down, you should be able to see your brand and get focused on your plan. Don't let the devil whisper negative talk into your ear. Please don't allow him to give you a sleeping pill to put you to sleep. He will try to provide you with anesthesia to cause a deep sleep. He wants to delay your progress. You must also realize that people will try to make you think your ideas, dreams, and goals are unimportant. Those things may not be necessary to some people, but please remember that they are vital to you and your target group. Trust me; you have people waiting to hear you.

You must keep yourself appropriate so that people are ready to listen to you. First, believe in yourself and what you have to say, and then others will believe in you. There's a Chinese proverb that says, "If you can command yourself, you can command the world." The Malaysian Institute recorded that managers who are stumbling over their weaknesses and misdoings will find it hard to convince others to improve. You must make sure you have your project and yourself all together before you can disperse the information that you have with others, especially if you want it to be successful.

The following story is often used as a metaphor for the inability or unwillingness of people to react to or be aware of threats that arise gradually rather than suddenly. I want to share it with you.

> Put a frog into a vessel filled with water on the stovetop and turn up the burner to start heating the water. As the temperature of the water begins to rise, the frog adjusts its temperature accordingly. The frog keeps adjusting its body temperature along with the increasing temperature of the water. Just when the water is about to reach its boiling point, the frog can no longer adjust. At this point the frog decides to jump out, but it's unable to do so because it has lost all its strength. Very soon, the frog dies.

What killed the frog? Think about it! I know many will say it was the boiling water. But the truth is the frog was killed by its own inability to jump out before it was too late.

We all need to adjust to people and situations, but we need to make sure we know when we need to adjust versus when we need to move on. There are times when we need to face the situation and take appropriate actions. If we allow people to exploit us physically, emotionally, financially, spiritually, or mentally, they will continue to do so. Let's decide when to jump! Let's jump while we still have strength.

Sometimes we allow ourselves to get into a calm and relaxed mode. We permit our inability and laziness to take over our minds; then, soon before we realize it, we have lost lots of valuable time just gazing at the clouds, doing nothing. We can't sit around day after day, giving up on our project and doing nothing. Time is precious, and we can't get it back when we lose it. Do not allow your time to slip through the hourglass.

I watched myself sit around and do nothing with my mission for years, and I had my mother and father on the sidelines trying to motivate me to get back with it. I felt I had lost heart, but I knew that I had to get done with the project set before me to get back in the game. There came a time in my life when I got so discouraged I felt like I had to put my project, goals, and mission on hold.

That particular season was full of distractions. This delay only caused me to come in during a later season. Sometimes if we don't move when God tells us to or when it is pressing on us, God allows other people to jump in line in front of us. Our ideas are fresher when God first gives them to us. So we must work while the daylight is upon us because no man can work when night comes.

CHAPTER EIGHT

The Planter

A S A BUSINESS OWNER, I PRACTICE PLANTING GOOD seeds in other businesses. In my definition, a planter often sows to see a harvest. A planter is not someone who plants into a business, a building, an event, or a person one time and never plants again. That's why the letters *-er* are on the end of the word *planter*—because it is an ongoing action.

A planter continues to plant, and a farmer continues to sow. That is how the increase continues to come. A prayer warrior prays all the time, and a singer sings often. They continue to function in their roles all the time, not just once.

Genesis 8:22 (KJV) states, "While the earth remaineth, seedtime and harvest, and cold and heat, and summer and winter, and day and night shall not cease." Galatians 6:7–9 (KJV) states, "Be not deceived; God is not mocked: for whatsoever a man soweth, that shall he also reap. For he that soweth to his flesh shall of the flesh reap corruption; but he that soweth to the Spirit shall of the Spirit reap life everlasting. And let us not be weary in doing well: for in due season we shall reap if we faint not."

These Bible verses help me realize that I need to continue sowing if I want to expect my harvest to be plentiful each year. These people have already established their brands as planters, sowers, or singers, and they have to continue working in their fields to make sure their brands are understood by others.

I have intentionally become a seed sower. I practice sowing seeds into other businesses, missions and projects every chance I get. I believe in biblical principles. I believe in the reaping and sowing principle. I know that a harvest will come back to me when I sow good or bad seeds. Therefore, practice sowing good seeds. I don't want to have a lack of reaping. I believe the harvest is always greater than the seed that's sown.

I know that when there are opportunities for me to plant seeds and I don't follow through, it could cause a lack in my harvested crops. What I mean by this is that if I want others to come to my events, I should show up at other speakers' events. Have you ever planted or noticed a garden that someone else has planted? When that crop comes up and is harvested, the planter must get prepared for the next season. He or she has to return the next year and plant another garden if there's to be a crop the following year.

It would help if you practiced planting good seeds several times during the year to experience good fruits coming up for you. The key is to plant in someone or something serious and trustworthy. Planting in good soil ensures a good return because the Bible speaks of reaping what you sow. That is how your increase will continue to come. In other words, you have to become a planter or a farmer—not of seeds in the ground but into the people, businesses, and others' projects.

A. How I Got My Business Started/ Planted

1. **Plant.** I planted my mission and vision in the soil of my heart—having a consulting business for women. I wrote my vision down and made it easy to remember and run with. I began to sow into my ministry by buying things I needed to help move my project along. I continue to work on making my mission better by purchasing a technical platform and online classes. I intentionally planted things that I wanted to come up. I sowed into others intentionally, especially the things I wanted to return to me. I invested in other

mentors' master classes, musical artists, and authors to become an effective leader and mentor.

2. **Water.** I had to water what I'd planted—my business. I had to keep it hydrated and alive. I had to keep my vision alive by constantly refreshing it and adding updates. I had to avoid depriving my garden of the essential things it needed to grow properly, like my attention to what was going on with it. Water is imperative to the growth of the crop. Leaves will dry up, and fruits and vegetables will not produce efficiently. You can apply this same analogy to your mission or project. It would help if you kept it watered and saturated. If not, your mission will cease, your dreams will vanish, and your goals will remain unaccomplished. Your vision will dry up and do nothing. If you deprive your project or mission of water, it will not have what it needs to survive. In this particular case, if you deprive yourself of wisdom, knowledge, and fresh ideas that you need to complete your mission; you will not have what you need to thrive. Suppose it comes to a halt. It would help if you gave it the things it needs most to survive or thrive.

3. **Wait.** I had to wait for God to give me the increase to see the business flourish. You will have to wait on your desired outcome. Wait for the plant to grow. Wait in good faith and hope. It shall come to pass. Let patience have its perfect work in the matter. One person plants, one waters, and God gives the increase.

First Corinthians 3:6–8 says, "I planted the seed, Apollos watered it, but God made it grow. So neither he who plants nor waters is anything, but only God, who makes things grow. The man who plants and the man who waters have one purpose, and each will be rewarded according to his labor."

Working on the work for my business:

A. Inspect. As my business started to grow, I watched it and continued to take preventive steps to make sure nothing was harming it like: negativity, not assessing its growth, or bare spots I've overlooked. Sometimes the farmer gets an empty place in his crop. He must chop that spot up again and replant before the season is over. A perfect reason he keeps a constant watch on the garden is to make sure it's growing properly. When you are working on your project, you have to continue to check to make sure there are no cracks or gaps in your work. If you discover gaps, you must correct and fix what's wrong, or you'll have missing parts.

B. Fertilize: During my process, I fertilized my business to help it grow. When my project required the extra boost and activation to help it thrive, I gave it new and fresher ideas. This helped enhance my growing and developing process. For example, when I needed to refresh videos for better sound and visual quality, I had to make my business better. I fertilized it when required. The farmer has to make sure the plant's growth is on target with how it's supposed to be growing. If the crop is not growing well, the farmer has to put fertilizer on it to help it grow. If your project is not coming together like it is supposed to for the particular stage, an extra boost will help. Many times this extra boost means praying for the business. Another means of help I used was to allow the help of my mentors with my project. I took these same steps that a farmer used and applied them to my vision of success. Remember, one has to keep planting in his garden to have something coming up each year. Your crop will not automatically come back by itself. You may have some voluntary things to spring up, but trust me, it won't come up as healthy, pretty, and complete as you'd like.

Sharing your crops with others is a pleasure when they've had the proper care. When you have successfully finished your product or mission, you will be happy and willing to share it with others. I am excited each time I share my information or products with others. When I worked on my project, it started as a seed and manifested just like a healthy plant in a garden does.

C. Insecticide. I also had to use the analogy of putting insecticide on my business by placing a protective cover or shield on it. When people tried to talk down to me or hate on me, I had to keep my business from being ruined or spoiled. I had to cut negative people off and disconnect myself from them. When I had nagging thoughts trying to block my project or destroy my vision, I had to quickly get rid of those things. The farmer has to make sure weeds aren't choking out or taking over his garden because he won't harvest much.

He wants to gather his expected crop. You can get all of the energy choked out of you on this journey. Don't let anyone steal your dreams. Don't let negative people get in your ears. You will know who they are when they start talking if you hadn't already spotted them out. Stay around positive people who are happy to see you moving forward. Stay around those who will support and see value in you. They will help keep you encouraged and moving forward.

CHAPTER NINE

Unchartered Water

W HEN YOU KEEP MOVING, EVEN WHEN YOU DON'T
know what lies ahead of you, God will allow you
to obtain and possess knowledge that will advance you to
another level—or should I say a fresh and new dimension
of your project, business, or mission. As you continue to
move through your process, you will grow and change. You

won't remain the same; you will improve and get better in the process.

As you pray and work, God will continue to give you revelations and knowledge that will improve your process. The more I worked on building my online classes, the more the Lord gave me new innovative ideas to continue building. Moving forward in this unchartered water was amazing, as I saw how God dropped so many ideas in my spirit to keep me busy working on my courses. It felt as though I had no limitations on how far I could go as long as I was moving forward with discipline and obedience to God.

Everything I've worked on or created centers around God and His biblical principles—my business, Christian conferences, tours, classes, and engagements. Unchartered waters are amazing. Have you ever been involved in a conversation or doing a speaking engagement where you had to produce information, answers, and messages that you knew little about? God will allow the Holy Spirit to step in and intervene in order to produce answers and information that you had no clue you possessed. Well, this kind of incident happened to me.

I spoke of my mentor Marshawn earlier. While attending one of her Speak for Pay workshops, I was called upon the stage with her as she worked on a brand makeover for me. Shaking in my boots, I stepped out and proceeded to the stage to have a brand makeover done. As I sat down on a stool that she had strategically placed right beside her on the stage, she proceeded to ask my name and what I did.

I spoke out to the audience and said, "My name is Kathy Hubbard, and I am a school teacher and a minister of Union Spring Baptist Church."

She then asked me if I was ready for a brand makeover.

I replied, "Yes, but I'm very nervous."

She said, "You want this right?"

And I said yes.

Let me say this before I go any farther. I already knew Marshawn would call me on stage that day. The Holy Spirit had already warned me. So just before Marshawn gave us a break from that morning session, I was frantically talking to my son who had attended this event with me. I was nervously rattling a piece of paper, trying to write some information about what I would say. Finally, my son convinced me that I needed to calm down and that it would be okay. We both went on break for lunch.

The whole time I was there, I had so much anxiety because I knew I'd be called on stage. After the break, Marshawn proceeded to give more notes for the second half of the conference. Finally, she got to the part for the brand makeovers. She pulled out a stack of papers to call the first name. I heard my name even before she called it.

Instantly after that, Marshawn said, "Kathy Hubbard."

My first reaction was, *Wow! I knew she was going to call me.* Yet I was still in shock. I paused in my seat before I could stand on my feet.

Then my son urged me, "Go on, Mother. Go on!"

As I walked down, totally lost in thought, Marshawn asked me, "What is it you would like to do?"

I replied, "I want to help women who are stuck in different life situations get unstuck. I want to empower them on how they can make it."

She asked me who I wanted to help and where.

I replied, "I want to help women of all walks of life. I would love doing women's conferences, retreats, and speaking in churches and organizations."

I told her that many women ask me to help them decide what they should do about certain situations.

Then I said, "Since I'm always helping, I wanted to have a business that specifically helps women."

I told her I wanted to speak in large churches like New Birth in Lithonia, Georgia, and Springfield Baptist Church in Conyers, Georgia.

Marshawn then asked me, "Have you ever considered speaking in colleges and schools to young women?"

I told her I hadn't, and she then suggested I should consider that and not limit myself.

She said, "Do you have something that all women need to hear?"

I said yes and then stated, "Well, I want to start an organization using the acronym WOMEN, which stands for *working on myself every day nonstop.*"

She said, "OK, this sounds like a radio talk show called *Everyday Women* since you want to help everyday women who are struggling."

When she said *everyday women*, a light bulb came on, and I got a clear idea for branding. I took this name and idea and ran with it and have been motivated ever since. I'm on track now, and I have been working hard every day since then. I have now officially changed my organization to Speak 180 Womentorial Consultant, Inc., a consulting and mentoring business for everyday WOMEN.

During another conference I attended with Marshawn, every participant was given a playbook to reference and follow along with as she taught her sessions. The playbook could also be used later to reference and help refresh knowledge of her teachings. It could assist in their efforts to work on branding and other projects. One of Marshawn's slogans in particular stuck out to me; she said that if we wait until we're completely ready, we may never get started at all. She said not to listen to the negative talk in your ears; you have to start before you're ready. She said we have to work on our project like a maverick.

My testimony is that God will help you if you are willing to help yourself. I started my mentoring group and leading women's conferences and became co-leader of the women's ministry at my home church. I have developed online classes to help stuck women get unstuck.

God will call you out by name from the back of the desert while holding your vision. You can't be afraid to speak out who God has called you to be. I am a witness to that. This particular incident reminds me of Joseph, the son of Jacob. Joseph had dreams, and during his life journey, he was able to walk out his destiny. Things didn't start to unravel until he spoke out to his family what he had dreamed.

I was hoping you could take how Joseph spoke to his family what he saw in his dream from the scriptures. He told about what God would allow him to do and what others in his dream were doing. Things begin happening to catapult Joseph into his destiny. A bad situation turned out to be the best thing that ever happened to Joseph. 'If you don't know the story of Joseph, please take the opportunity to read it in Genesis 37–50 to learn more.

I'd begun working and searching for ways I could become who God had called me to be, and one day during a snowstorm, I randomly pulled Marshawn up on the internet, but I realized that she was divinely set before me to inspire me to get out of the rut and to allow God to catapult me toward my destiny. I thank God often for visiting me on this matter and strategically placing Marshawn in my life. I hope and trust that I can help direct you in the same manner. I want you to know that your breakthrough is closer than you think.

When you want to give up, you better hold on, strap your boots up, and get ready, because it is right around the corner. I tell you, I was just as close as you are to giving up. But I muscled up enough strength to give my dreams another try, and that is right where God was for me. He has been making a way for me ever since. So I encourage you to hang in there and go on to birth the vision that God has given you.

You are not too late, old, or weak. You are sufficiently

ready. God has equipped you with everything you need to birth whatever it is you are supposed to deliver. Remain focused. The late Dr. Myles Munroe stated, "All of us came to this earth because there is something that the earth needed that God put inside of us. Everything in creation was created with a gift. We were sent here to the earth by a greater power to deliver something that the people need. We owe the people something, and we are carrying it." I encourage you to find out what you are carrying, so you can work on it and give the world what they are waiting on.

CHAPTER TEN

Time to Play

IT IS NOW TIME TO ROLL WITH IT. I AM DOING EXACTLY that—rolling with it. God is so good, as he allows me to move with it. So many doors have opened for me during this process, including television airtime, working on the production of a single album, branding materials, networking connections, creating online classes, and more—including this book, *Release the Pause Button*. God is faithful, and I expect him to do exceedingly and abundantly great things with me. My dream is flourishing, and I am so happy I decided to stop procrastinating and move forward with my mission. I will continue to stick to the plan and allow God to pour into me as I give others information on how to get through this process.

I once heard my mentor Marshawn Evans say, "Many are called, but few are chosen." Then she proceeded to state, "Yes, many are called, but the ones who are chosen are the ones who choose to get up and answer the call."

Thanks to God for choosing me and giving me this opportunity to work as a chosen vessel. I now enjoy helping young girls and women and anyone who feels stuck. I enjoy speaking, singing, preaching, and empowering everyday women to achieve their expected potential. I encourage you to roll with the process God has given you and work on dreams and goals; it is now time to get those things done. People are waiting on you.

When you pull your project together and begin to use it and reach out to others, you will find that your plans, dreams, and visions are not only important to you, but to someone else as well. They are waiting on you to see what you have to say and what you can offer. Whatever you plan to produce, make sure it includes your brand. Make sure your brand is the best one you can create for yourself.

When you begin to press play and roll with it, you will have the opportunity to listen to and evaluate yourself. You will be so pleased to find how your gift operates. You will be surprised to see how everything will come together to make you become the best you can be.

As Marshawn says, "Start before you are ready." If you start before you are ready, you will have the essential pieces you need when you're ready. During the process, there are things you may not have a clear understanding of, but continue to work toward your mission and build, and you will find that those pieces are necessary to complete the process. You will be able to put an excellent project together if you can work on one vision at a time. God will strategically put you in place when it is time to play. Don't worry; it will all come together.

Life Is Great

You can have a great successful life if you choose to step up to the challenge. You can achieve and do whatever you apply yourself to. You can't be what you want if you sit on your seat doing nothing. You have to make it happen.

Your brand can be and will be just what you make it. You have to live up to the standard of your brand. When you brand yourself and do an excellent job with the process, it will help you figure out how to continue with your overall project.

During your life journey, you have to evaluate what you have done, what you are doing, and what you want to do in the future. Doing this will help you find your purpose and align you closer to your destiny. When you figure out what you're doing that is drawing you closer to who you believe you're supposed to be, you have to focus on that and capitalize on it to brand your business.

Drawing closer to my purpose helped me create my brand. I am a minister of music in my home church, which is a leadership position. I am a preacher of God's Word, so others look to me as a leader. I love working to help women, youth, and coaching. These titles give me the credibility to believe in myself as a leader. I have also studied and earned a doctor of biblical ministry degree. I have a specialist's degree in leadership and administration. Compiling all of these things leads me toward leadership and coaching. Therefore, I know I'm a leader, and I can teach, consult, and coach women to help them figure out what their brands may be.

I have credentials, experiences, skills, and the ability to work on your behalf as a mentor or consultant. My job is to help encourage women to work on themselves nonstop and get unstuck from procrastination every day. Therefore, my suggestion is to begin applying work to your mission every day. When you find yourself working to improve in a particular area of your life, and it seems like everything you're doing centers around what you are working on, focus on that area. That should be a clue that you are driven in a direction that you should probably pay more attention to so that you walk in your purpose.

I want to mentor you in the right direction and help you work on your process until you've completed the mission.

You may be working on yourself, improving family skills, working on a project or goal, or something else. I am here to help you. As you work on your task and move closer to the result, I will help you figure out what you are doing to develop your brand, which will eventually lead you to your trademark. You will be able to get started with whatever it is you're seeking to do.

CHAPTER ELEVEN

Living the Purpose

GOD'S WILL FOR YOUR LIFE IS THAT YOU LIVE A purpose-filled, carefully planned life. If you choose to not step up to the plate, you will continue living beneath where God destined you to live. You have to dream, record, produce, read, and live on the level where God has ordained you to be. You know it is in you; all you have to do is have faith and work through the process to completion.

There have been so many times when I got complacent, lazy, and tired of trying to make things work. Believe me when I say that I made many attempts and also paused. All I got from it was an unfinished product. I have now released the pause button and encourage you to do the same. I promise you I was once held hostage by procrastination, but I made the big decision to move forward and not look back.

I can genuinely say that I have worked hard on this process to finish my product this time. Since I made it to this season, I believe this is the time when God will allow me to flourish. I know that God is ready for me to come into full blossom because he has enabled me to do my work efficiently and effectively.

I am now walking in my destiny, and I don't feel like anybody could hold me down, because he has made my way plain. If you trust in his plan he will do the same for you. Traveling this road to my destiny was never short of being busy and long but enjoyable and fulfilling. Hence, as I press my way through this process while patiently waiting and seeking God's face, I realize I am walking in my destiny.

I received prophetic words from two individuals who I couldn't forget during the process. One word, which was *God*, has put me on a fast track to a victorious life in him, and from that instant, I started praying, fasting, reading, journaling, and writing songs. What I thought was a fast track was a slow pace to me, but to God, it was quick.

The next word I received was a word confirming my destiny to work with women in a large capacity. I have received many encouraging and prophetic words from preachers, my parents, my brother and sister, and others. My parents and family members have stood beside me and have believed in me from day one. I appreciate that because we all need someone who will trust and believe in us, just as we believe in ourselves. Lastly, as you follow me, I will provide you with material to help you start your process.

Below is a short questionnaire/survey to help outline the action plan for your project. Answer the questions below and use this as a guideline to help you get through your project.

1. Write your story. Your story should be catchy and tell of an obstacle or hurt or outstanding achievement you have experienced.

2. Could your story possibly lead you to a potential business pursuit? When you tell your story, is it the reason you want to pursue your project?

3. How could your story be narrowed down to a brand that becomes a mission to pursue?

4. What's stopping you from pursuing your mission or project? For example, are you procrastinating because of a lack of resources or moral support?

1.

2.

3.

4.

5. If you are willing to push through your obstacles, list a few ways you could take to accomplish your goals.

6. Identify yourself in the process: are you in the beginning, middle, or are you stuck on pause instead of completing your project?

7. What do you want your project outcome to resemble? (Destination)

8. After reading this book, how do you plan to take steps to finish?

    1.

    2.

    3.

    4.

9. How has this book inspired you to get started, unstuck, and complete your project?

    1.

    2.

    3.

    4.

10. On a scale of 1 to 10, how helpful was this book? For example, one is not helpful, and ten is extremely helpful.

1–2 Not helpful

3–4 A little helpful

5–6 Somewhat helpful

7–8 Helpful

9–10 Extremely helpful

CHAPTER TWELVE

Transformation Since COVID-19

SINCE THE UNWANTED ENTRANCE OF COVID-19, OUR world has taken a huge turn. People have passed away or been very ill, and many are carrying symptoms of this virus. This virus has ripped our nation and our hearts apart, along with the economy, businesses, families, schools, organizations, and more. There have been so many horror stories. Since this virus hit, people have been dealing with depression, anxiety, poverty, abuse, confusion, physical, and psychological problems.

Needless to say, as of January of 2022, we are still being affected by the coronavirus. Life during this pandemic, protests, and this problematic election has been depressing. The country has gone through a lot. It is challenging for the government to focus and move forward. It has been a callous time for all of us. I hope this book has inspired you to work as hard as I have to give you the road map to complete your project.

To turn your dreams into a successful career, you must get unstuck. I've noticed that so many women aspire to accomplish their dreams, goals, or mission, but they are stuck. When women are chasing a dream, often many sacrifices are needed. The sacrifices usually include more energy, competency, economic resources, and support; however, the same sacrifices are necessary for men—though men tend to push and pursue their dreams at a higher rate than women.

I read a study showing that many women should be realistic, stop dreaming, get their heads out of the clouds, play it safe, and not take chances. As a result, the challenges of achieving dreams may appear more complex and unrealistic, and women start to become less ambitious. However; I want to encourage women to keep pushing through your process. You can accomplish your dreams and mission.

Focus on the New You

You may not see it or feel it, but the new way of life since COVID-19 has opened many doors for everyday women and people with a plan or dream. You can start with an online course, conferences, parties, retreats, talk shows, networking membership sales, and more. Working from home or anywhere in the world is available for you. The environment may not be a good time and season to get out and work in the community, but it is a perfect time to get on your computer, phone, or internet and work your butt off.

The sky is the limit. Now is the perfect time to be seen. You should know your stuff because there are many people out there trying to embark on a new adventure, and you want something that will set you apart from others. I listened to a message given by the late Myles Munroe on understanding the principles of self-manifestation.

Munroe stated, "People are not looking for you, but they are looking for what you are carrying. If you do not manifest what you are carrying, the world will ignore you." He also said, "Because you exist doesn't mean you are going to be successful. Most humans live on earth and never manifest themselves. You can die, and people will never know that you were here. The most important goal should be self-manifestation" (https://youtu.be/2ZD2e3u1KeQ).

The reality is I had gone from year to year saying I was going to do something and that I'd walk in my calling, but I would let that year slip right by me without getting it done. Myles Munroe says in the video it's because I tolerated what I was allowing to happen. That is a powerful statement. He said discontent is the seed of change. Then he goes on to say, "You will never change what you tolerate." I encourage you to listen to this video on YouTube (https://youtu. be/2ZD2e3u1KeQ). I have been so enlightened by many mentors and leaders during this downtime. I've learned things that I would not have gained if I had not taken this rest time from work.

My mindset is different, and you have to change your mindset if you plan to get your work done. Now is a perfect time to apply this scripture to our lives. Romans 12:2 (KJV) says, "And be not conformed to this world but be ye transformed by the renewing of your mind." I can tell everyone that, but until you do it yourself, you will be in the same place.

My mind thinks differently from yours, and your mind thinks differently from mine. Therefore you have to renew your mind to get yourself up and embrace the new you. Work to make your dreams come true. Steve Harvey said, "Your dream has to be so big that it dwarfs all your fears." You need to have a dream, plan, or mission. Go after it with all your might and it will come to pass. I can't say this enough that time waits on no one.

It doesn't matter if you consider yourself as small or large, intelligent or not, rich or poor—time waits on no one. If you are new or old, you have an opportunity to move forward during this precedent time, so please jump in and get on top of your game. If you wait, you will be a veteran, and this time and season may pass you by. If that happens, you'll have to wait for another season. Therefore jump in and get your homework done.

Finally, there are 8 key steps to an action-plan that I developed, which will help you move through your process to completion. These steps are shared in more details in my mini course. The steps are:

1. Write It
2. Believe It
3. Create It
4. Share It
5. Learn It
6. Teach It
7. Launch It
8. Pitch It

Thank you for letting me share this information with you on how to release the pause button, stop procrastinating, get unstuck and begin earning bucks, if that is your desire.

SOURCES

1   Daniels, Marshawn Evans, Mentor.

2   Jakes, T.D., Quote.

3   Kafele, Baruti, Mentor.

4   Holy Bible, King James Version.

5   Lee, Bruce, Quote: Https://libquotes.com.

6   Leslie, Danielle, Mentor

7   Maltz, Maxwell: https://www.goodreads.com/quotes/1176507-what-is-opportunity-and-when-does-it-knock-it-never.

8   Mason, Babbie, Mentor.

10 Monroe, Myles, Steve Harvey and Denzel Washington, Video: "Understanding the Principles of Self Manifestation." https://youtu.be/2ZD2e3u1KeQ.

11 New International Version. Bible Gateway. Web. January 29, 2015.

12 Quinn's, Daniel. "The Story of B." "The Boiling Frog, Excerpt from the book."

13 The Life Application Bible: Kings James Version. Wheaton, IL. Tyndale House Publishing, Inc.

14 Malaysian Institute of Management in 2012-04-21. http://www360doc.com.

Printed in the United States
by Baker & Taylor Publisher Services